OHIO

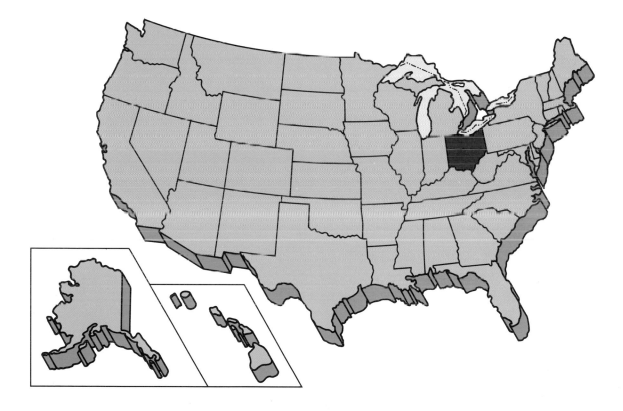

Hello U★S★A★

OHIO

Dottie Brown

THE GREAT SEAL OF THE STATE OF OHIO

Lerner Publications Company

This book is available in two editions:
Library binding by Lerner Publications Company
Soft cover by First Avenue Editions
241 First Avenue North
Minneapolis, MN 55401
ISBN: 0–8225–2725–1 (lib. bdg.)
ISBN: 0–8225–9708–X (pbk.)

LIBRARY OF CONGRESS
CATALOGING-IN-PUBLICATION DATA
Brown, Dottie.
    Ohio / Dottie Brown.
      p.   cm. — (Hello USA)
    Includes index.
    Summary: Introduces Ohio's history, geog-
raphy, economy, and environmental concerns.
    ISBN 0–8225–2725–1 (lib. bdg.)
    1. Ohio—Juvenile literature.
[1. Ohio.] I. Title. II. Series.
F491.3.B76 1992
977.1—dc20   91–38390
                    CIP
                    AC

Cover photograph courtesy
of Hank Andrews/Visuals
Unlimited.

The glossary that begins on
page 68 gives definitions of
words shown in **bold type** in
the text.

Manufactured in the United States of America
3 4 5 6 7 – JR – 99 98 97 96

 This book is printed
on acid-free, recyla-
ble paper.

CONTENTS

Buzzard

Did You Know . . . ?

☐ Every year on March 15 a flock of buzzards heading north for the summer flies into Hinckley, Ohio. The people of Hinckley celebrate the arrival of the birds with a festival on Buzzard Day, the first Sunday after March 15.

☐ In 1869 the Cincinnati Red Stockings became the first professional baseball team in the United States.

☐ Ohio is known as the Mother of Presidents. Seven U.S. presidents —Ulysses S. Grant, Rutherford B. Hayes, James Garfield, Benjamin

Harrison, William McKinley, William Howard Taft, and Warren Harding—were born in the state.

❏ John Glenn, the first American to orbit the earth in a spaceship, and Neil Armstrong, the first person to walk on the moon, were both from Ohio.

❏ Ohio produces more tomatoes than any state except California.

❏ Between 1870 and the mid-1900s, more rubber tires were made in Akron, Ohio, than in any other place in the world. The city was once known as the Rubber Capital of the World.

A Trip Around the State

The state of Ohio takes its name from the wide river that forms its southern and southeastern borders. The Iroquois Indians called this river *oheo,* meaning "beautiful." Another great body of water —Lake Erie, one of the five **Great Lakes**—shapes Ohio's northern border.

Michigan also lies north of Ohio. Pennsylvania and West Virginia border Ohio on the east, Kentucky is to the south, and Indiana is to the west.

More than 20,000 years ago, water in the form of **glaciers** shaped Ohio's land regions. These huge sheets of ice crept over two-thirds of what is now Ohio, gouging out lake beds and scraping off hilltops. When the glaciers melted, they left a thick carpet of **till** (ground-up rocks and dirt) behind.

One region in Ohio has so much till that it is called the Till Plains. The state's other regions are the Appalachian Plateau, the Bluegrass Region, and the Lake Plains.

9

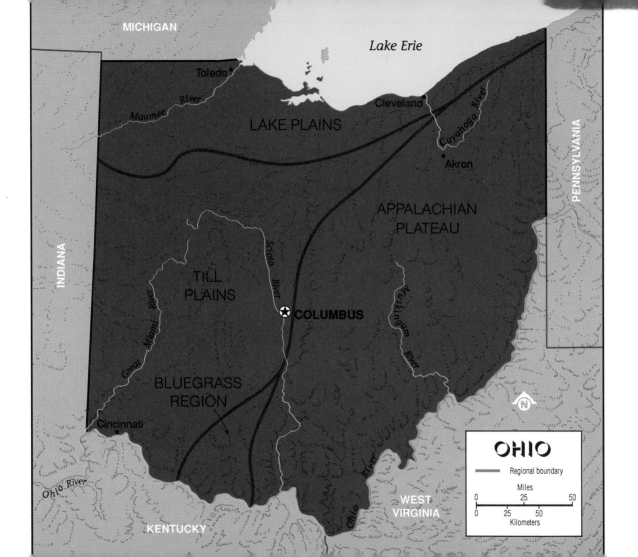

MICHIGAN

Lake Erie

Toledo

Maumee River

LAKE PLAINS

Cleveland

Cuyahoga River

Akron

PENNSYLVANIA

APPALACHIAN
PLATEAU

INDIANA

Scioto River

TILL
PLAINS

COLUMBUS

Muskingum River

Great Miami River

BLUEGRASS
REGION

Cincinnati

Ohio River

Ohio River

KENTUCKY

WEST
VIRGINIA

N

OHIO

Regional boundary

Miles
0   25   50

0   25   50
Kilometers

Steep cliffs tower over visitors at Hocking Hills State Park in the Appalachian Plateau.

The gently rolling Till Plains blanket most of western Ohio. This region contains some of the best farmland in the nation. Low hills stand in the southern Till Plains. One of these, Campbell Hill, is Ohio's highest point.

The Appalachian Plateau covers eastern Ohio. Glaciers moved over only the northern third of the region, smoothing it out and leaving the fertile soil that is now used for farming. Tree-covered hills, deep valleys, and jagged ridges lie south of this farmland. Buried under the **plateau,** or highland, are deposits of coal, oil, clay, and salt.

11

The Bluegrass Region, a small triangle of land in southern Ohio, is wedged between the Till Plains and the Appalachian Plateau. Flat-topped hills dot the Bluegrass Region.

The Lake Plains cut a path across northern Ohio. This region, which holds two of the state's largest cities, borders Lake Erie. A forested swamp once filled the western end of the Lake Plains. In the late 1800s, Ohioans drained the swamp and planted crops there. It is still excellent farmland, as is much of the land in this region.

Pike Lake, which lies in the Bluegrass Region, offers fishing, boating, and swimming.

The Lake Plains region has many cities, including Cleveland *(above)*, as well as fertile farmland.

The oldest lighthouse on Lake Erie guides ships around Marblehead Peninsula.

Lake Erie's shoreline extends 312 miles (502 kilometers) across northern Ohio. The lake is linked to the Saint Lawrence Seaway, a waterway that connects the Great Lakes to the Atlantic Ocean. The seaway allows Ohioans to ship goods from Lake Erie to markets around the world.

The Ohio River has been a valuable water highway for thousands of years. The Great Miami, Scioto, and Muskingum rivers flow into the Ohio. Other rivers in Ohio, including the Cuyahoga and the Maumee, travel northward into Lake Erie.

Plenty of rain and snow, about 38 inches (97 centimeters) a year, feeds Ohio's rivers. Winter temperatures in the state average 28° F

Ice-cold water rushes through a forest.

(–2° C). Summer temperatures average 73° F (23° C). Tornadoes sometimes twist through Ohio in the spring and fall.

In the fall, leaves throughout Ohio turn brilliant red, yellow, and orange.

Ohio's warm summers and plentiful rainfall allow many kinds of plants to grow. In the spring, black-eyed Susans, buttercups, and other wildflowers push through the soil. Though settlers cut down many of Ohio's forests to plant crops, large stands of oak, hickory, beech, maple, and sycamore trees still cover about one-fourth of the state.

At one time, wolves, bears, buffalo, and deer roamed through Ohio. But the white-tailed deer is the only large animal still thriving in Ohio's countryside. Red foxes, woodchucks, and rabbits also live in the state's forests.

Barn swallows perch on a wire *(above)*. Crab apple trees blossom in the spring *(right)*.

Ohio's Story

Nearly 13,000 years ago, the first people came to the Ohio area. The ancestors of these ancient Native Americans, or Indians, had probably reached North America by crossing a land bridge that once connected Asia to North America.

The Indians speared beavers as large as bears and huge mastodons —hairy elephants with great tusks. Over time, these large animals disappeared, and the Indians' descendants began to hunt bears and deer and gather berries, nuts, and roots. By 800 B.C., a group of Indians called mound builders had replaced the hunters and gatherers.

The mound builders put their dead in tombs and heaped layers of dirt on the graves, forming mounds of earth. The Indians built other mounds for religious ceremonies. Many of the ceremonial mounds were shaped like animals.

The Great Serpent Mound, so called because it looks like a huge snake, is 1,330 feet (405 meters) long.

This skeleton was found buried deep in a mound in southwestern Ohio.

By around A.D. 1600, the mound builders had vanished. No one knows for sure what happened to them, but they may have starved when droughts, or long dry spells, caused their crops to fail.

About 100 years later, new groups of Indians moved into what is now Ohio. The Shawnee, Miami, and Wyandot were pushed into the area by other tribes. People from Great Britain formed **colonies** (settlements) on the eastern coast of North America, driving the Delaware Indians into Ohio too.

The Indians built their villages along rivers. They fished, gathered wild berries, nuts, and grapes, and planted crops of corn, beans, and tobacco. They also hunted deer, mink, beaver, and fox.

The tribes traded the furs from these animals to the French and British, who had set up trading posts in the region to do business with the Indians. The French and British exchanged kettles, blankets, guns, and other European goods for the furs.

The skin of a male deer, called a buckskin, was worth one dollar to fur traders. Buckskin got shortened to buck, a word which eventually came to mean a dollar bill.

Soon France and Britain each wanted the land and fur trade in North America for themselves. The two countries went to war in 1754. By 1763 the British had gained control of a large area that included what is now Ohio.

But the British did not have this land for long. The 13 colonies wanted to be free from British control, so they went to war with Britain. In 1783 the colonists won the war, called the American Revolution, and formed their own country—the United States of America. In just a few years, settlers had moved into the new country's Northwest Territory, which included present-day Ohio. The settlers built Marietta, the first permanent white settlement in Ohio.

To clear space for crops, early settlers killed trees by cutting deep gashes in them. Later, settlers chopped down the trees and burned the dead trunks.

As more white settlers came to the territory, the Indians living in the region grew angry. The newcomers were pushing the tribes out of the area, just as the colonists had pushed the Delaware out of the East. So the Indians fought to keep their land, attacking settlements.

The U.S. government sent soldiers to stop the Indian attacks. Miami chief Little Turtle and his warriors, who came from several tribes, won two important battles, but U.S. troops eventually outnumbered and overpowered the Indians.

After U.S. troops won the Battle of Fallen Timbers in 1794, the Shawnee, Miami, Delaware, and Wyandot Indians lost most of their land to pioneers.

Settlers land at what is now Cincinnati.

In 1795 the weakened Indians gave up about two-thirds of what is now Ohio. Gradually, the U.S. government squeezed the Indians into a small corner of the region, then pushed them out entirely.

No longer fearing Indian attacks, settlers began to pour into the area. Soon enough people had arrived for the area to qualify for statehood. On March 1, 1803, Ohio was carved out of the Northwest Territory and became the 17th state.

About 70,000 Ohioans lived in the new state. Many were farmers who needed to get their crops and livestock to market quickly. But the few roads that existed were rough and took weeks to travel. Crops could easily spoil before they reached their destination—if they got there at all.

The Hinckley Hunt

Farming in the 1800s was hard work. Settlers had to cut crops and carry them to the barn by hand. Storing the harvest was not easy, either. Squirrels ate wheat out of barns and stole vegetables from gardens. Wolves killed chickens and hogs.

To get rid of the animals, the town of Hinckley, Ohio, held a hunt on Christmas Eve, 1818. More than 500 hunters encircled the town. Then they moved inward, killing every animal in sight. At the end of the day, the hunters divided up the bounty and took it home to eat.

Sailors push a keelboat.

Ohioans used rivers as highways to transport their goods. The Ohio River, because it flows through many states, was an especially important trade route.

At first, keelboats carried the crops. Keelboats were long boats with sails. The river current took the keelboat downriver quickly, but the boat's crew had to push the boat all the way back upriver using long poles.

In 1811 steamboats appeared on the Ohio River. With their steam-powered paddles and large storage spaces, steamboats could carry more crops faster than keelboats. By 1825 steamboats had begun to travel the Erie Canal, a canal connecting Lake Erie to the Hudson River in New York. Ohio's farmers now had a direct water route to the large markets of New York City.

The Ohio and Erie Canal *(above)* stretched for many miles. On one side of the canal was a towpath. Horses walked on the path and pulled small boats along the canal at about four miles (six km) per hour. Once the boats reached the end of the canal, their cargo was put on a steamboat *(left),* which carried the goods to market.

Workers in Cincinnati's meat-packing plants butchered and cleaned about 1,500 hogs a day.

Ohio's population soon swelled to nearly 1.5 million. In 1839 the state led the nation in wheat production. And by 1850, Ohio ranked first in horse and sheep population.

Hog and dairy farming became important too. Workers in Cincinnati slaughtered and packed so many hogs—more than 400,000 a year—that the city was called Porkopolis.

Ohio's natural resources helped industry develop rapidly in the state. For example, the state's strong river currents powered mills, which ground farmers' corn and wheat into meal and flour.

Woodworkers crafted furniture, barrels, and wagons from Ohio's trees. Potters made dishes and jugs out of clay found in the state. Miners chiseled tons of coal out of the earth to power steam engines.

In the mid-1800s, many pottery factories were built near clay deposits in eastern and south central Ohio.

Ohio's industries created jobs that drew thousands of people to the state, including slaves who had escaped from the South, where slavery was legal. When the U.S. government passed laws making it hard for former slaves to remain safely in Ohio, many Ohioans helped the runaways flee to Canada, where the slave owners could not legally chase them. The system that helped escaped slaves reach a safe place was called the **Underground Railroad**.

Escaped slaves often crossed the Ohio River on their way from the South to Ohio, where slavery was illegal.

The Ohioans who ran the Underground Railroad, as well as many people throughout the country, wanted to outlaw slavery in every state. In 1861 several Southern states withdrew from the Union to form a separate country where slavery would remain legal. To keep the Union together, the North fought against the South in what became known as the Civil War. Nearly 350,000 Ohioans helped the North win the war by 1865.

The Underground Railroad

In 1852 Harriet Beecher Stowe wrote *Uncle Tom's Cabin*. This book described the cruelty of slavery and the desperate attempts slaves made to escape. Stowe based the book on true stories she had heard from escaped slaves while she lived in Cincinnati. Stowe's powerful book, which sold millions of copies, convinced many people that slavery was wrong.

Some Ohioans who agreed with Stowe were part of the Underground Railroad. They hid escaped slaves in wagons, canal boats, trains, barns, and homes. The slaves usually traveled at night to avoid being caught. If they were captured and returned to their owners, slaves would not only lose their freedom, they were also likely to be severely punished. People who helped escaped slaves risked going to jail.

After the war, Ohio's industries continued to grow. Railroads were one reason for this success. Ohio farmers and merchants could send their goods quickly by railroad all across the country. Thousands of miles of railroad tracks stretched through Ohio.

Natural resources, especially coal, oil, and natural gas, also continued to be a key to Ohio's industrial success. Most factories and railroads depended on these fuels to power their machinery. Because Ohio had plenty of fuel, it was cheap and drew industries to the state from all over the country.

One of these was the rubber industry. In 1870 Benjamin F. Goodrich moved his rubber factory from New York to Akron. At first the factory made fire hoses, but it soon produced tires for the cars and trucks made in Ohio and in nearby Michigan.

Railroads *(left)* carried oil from western Ohio to factories in Cleveland *(above)*, where the oil was cleaned and sent on to other states.

Steel was another important industry. Ships on Lake Erie brought iron ore to Ohio, where the metal was used to make steel. The state's steel industry grew to be the second largest in the country.

Ohio inventors created even more industries. In 1903 Wilbur and Orville Wright, bicycle mechanics from Dayton, Ohio, made the first successful flight in an airplane. Their work encouraged other people around the world to design and build more aircraft.

The Day Dayton Drowned

Before dams were built to control flooding, Ohioans expected floods. The Ohio River spilled over its banks almost every spring. During the winter, blocks of ice often backed up the state's northern rivers, causing more flooding. But the flood of 1913 was Ohio's worst. Three days of pouring rain swelled rivers to overflowing. Almost every city in Ohio near a river flooded, killing nearly 500 people. Dayton was hardest hit. Twenty feet of water covered its downtown area, and businesses lost hundreds of millions of dollars in property damage.

When the United States entered World War I in 1917, Ohio's industries got even busier. Workers made rubber, airplanes, and parts for cars and trucks, all of which were needed to fight the war. When the war ended, however, so did the high demand for Ohio's

During World War I, many farmers sent their crops to soldiers in Europe, so food was often scarce in the United States. Women in Cincinnati helped feed Ohioans by planting gardens on vacant lots in the city.

Almost half of all factory workers in Ohio lost their jobs during the Great Depression. Many people depended on money from the government to survive. Here, Clevelanders wait in line for government aid.

products. Factories closed, and in Akron alone, 50,000 people lost their jobs.

Then the Great Depression, a time when many banks and businesses shut down, hit the country in 1929. The depression, which lasted through the 1930s, left many Americans without jobs or money. More factories closed and many of Ohio's farmers lost their land.

While men fought in World War II, many women made bombs, torpedoes, trucks, and tanks. Although few industries had hired women before the war, some factories had all-female crews during the war.

Ohio's industries started up again in 1941, when the United States entered World War II. Workers again built ships, airplanes, and weapons. Farmers grew tons of grain to feed the soldiers fighting overseas. A company in Toledo made jeeps for the troops, while other factories made huge tanks.

After the war ended in 1945, Ohio continued to prosper. The

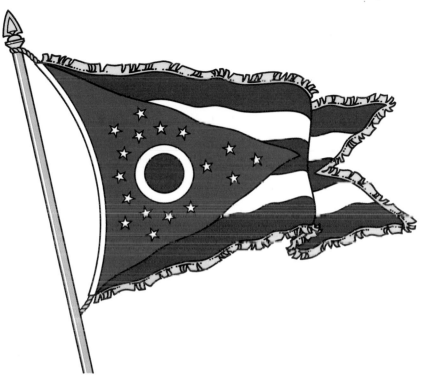

Ohio has the only state flag in the country that is shaped like a swallow's tail. The white circle is an 'O' for Ohio, and the red center of the 'O' stands for the nut of the buckeye, Ohio's state tree.

state's population grew, and almost everyone who needed to earn money could find a job. But by the end of the 1970s, some of Ohio's industries had moved to states where the costs of running a business were lower. These industries took thousands of jobs with them.

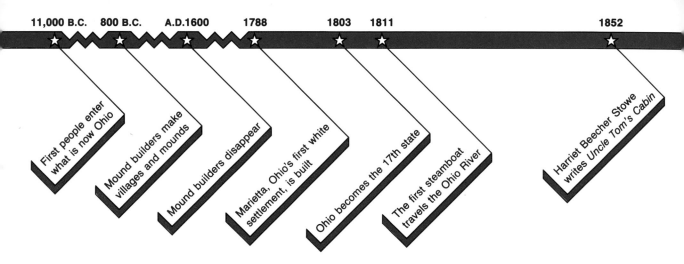

| 11,000 B.C. | 800 B.C. | A.D.1600 | 1788 | 1803 | 1811 | 1852 |

First people enter what is now Ohio

Mound builders make villages and mounds

Mound builders disappear

Marietta, Ohio's first white settlement, is built

Ohio becomes the 17th state

The first steamboat travels the Ohio River

Harriet Beecher Stowe writes *Uncle Tom's Cabin*

The 1970s and 1980s were hard for Ohio, but the state has learned from its difficulties. Ohioans are working in many ways—lowering taxes, building new office buildings, and making new highways—to keep the state's industries strong and attract new businesses.

40

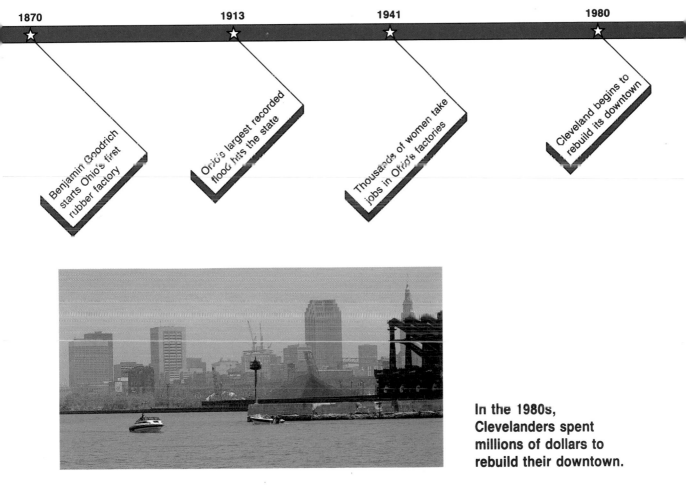

1870 — Benjamin Goodrich starts Ohio's first rubber factory

1913 — Ohio's largest recorded flood hits the state

1941 — Thousands of women take jobs in Ohio's factories

1980 — Cleveland begins to rebuild its downtown

In the 1980s, Clevelanders spent millions of dollars to rebuild their downtown.

41

Columbus

Living and Working in Ohio

When it comes to people, Ohio is a giant. With more than 10.5 million residents, Ohio ranks seventh in population in the United States. But the state is not large in terms of land—33 states are larger.

About three-fourths of all Ohioans live in cities. The state's largest cities are Columbus (the capital), Cleveland, and Cincinnati. Ohio has seven cities with populations over 500,000. Only California has more large cities.

At Oktoberfest in Ohio, German Americans dress, eat, and dance the same way their ancestors did in Germany.

Almost all Ohioans were born in the United States, but their ancestors came from around the world. Many sailed from Great Britain. Others came later from Germany, Italy, Poland, Greece, Hungary, and elsewhere in Europe. A little more than 10 percent of Ohio's people are African American. Hispanics, Native Americans, and Asians together only make up about 3 percent of the state's population.

Ohioans are proud of their educational system. Oberlin College was the first in the nation to educate men and women together. And Wilberforce University was the first U.S. college for African-American students.

On hot summer days, some Ohioans play in the fountain area at Serpentine Wall in Cincinnati.

Airplane fans in Ohio can see World War II bombers, as well as an Apollo space capsule, at the huge U.S. Air Force Museum near Dayton. History buffs can visit Roscoe Village, a town on the Ohio and Erie Canal rebuilt to look just like it did in the 1830s. As visitors walk alongside the Great Serpent Mound in southwestern Ohio, they can imagine what Ohio was like in the days of the mound builders.

A batter for the Cleveland Indians awaits the pitch.

Sports enthusiasts will find plenty to watch in Ohio. Two professional baseball teams play in the state—the Cincinnati Reds and the Cleveland Indians. Ohio is also home to two pro football teams, the Cincinnati Bengals and the Cleveland Browns, and one basketball team, the Cleveland Cavaliers.

For people who prefer doing to watching, Ohio offers lots of choices. Canoeists can glide down the hundreds of miles of rivers and creeks in the state. The Wayne National Forest, which covers a large part of southeastern Ohio, has wilderness trails for those who want to hike. Thrill seekers can ride the roller coasters at popular amusement parks such as Kings Island near Cincinnati or Cedar Point in Sandusky.

The Witches Wheel at Cedar Point spins its riders into the air.

Most service jobs are in cities *(above)*. But some service workers, like the captain of a ferryboat on Lake Erie *(right),* travel Ohio's waterways.

Service jobs employ more than two-thirds of Ohio's workers. People who work for restaurants, hospitals, banks, schools, and the government have service jobs. The greatest number of service workers in Ohio sell and trade items such as food, coal, cars, and steel. Other service workers move these products into and out of Ohio by ship, river barge, railroad, airplane, or truck. Almost two-thirds of the money earned in Ohio comes from services.

About one-fourth of Ohio's workers manufacture products. Workers at metal foundries make steel that is sold across the nation. Within Ohio, some of the steel is used to mold parts for cars, trucks, airplanes, washing machines, and air conditioners. Ohio workers assemble cars and trucks. Rubber companies make tires in Akron and Cleveland. And the largest soap factory in the United States is in Cincinnati.

A factory worker assembles an airplane engine.

Ohioans also prepare lots of different foods. In Cincinnati, workers pack meat. In Columbus, workers brew beer and bake breads and pastries. Tuscarawas, a county in eastern Ohio, makes so much Swiss cheese that it has been nicknamed Little Switzerland.

Only a small number of Ohioans farm for a living. Farmers make just 1 percent of the money earned in Ohio. The two main crops are corn and soybeans. Farmers also grow large crops of cucumbers, tomatoes, and wheat.

Warm breezes from Lake Erie

Apple trees thrive in Ohio, where Johnny Appleseed once planted thousands of apple seeds.

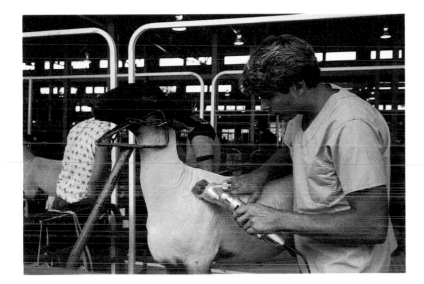

A sheep waits while its wool is sheared, or shaved off.

help protect fruit crops in northern Ohio from frost in spring and fall. As a result, many farmers are able to grow grapes and strawberries.

Ohio is a leading producer of hogs. Farmers in southwestern Ohio raise hogs to sell to meat-packing plants in Cincinnati, where the hogs are butchered and packaged to be sold in supermarkets. Dairy cattle graze on farms in southeastern Ohio. Livestock farmers in other areas of the state raise sheep and poultry.

Some of the limestone mined in central Ohio goes into cement, which is used to make buildings, sidewalks, and roads.

Very few Ohioans are miners. But these few people remove millions of tons of coal from the earth every year. Other miners dig for salt and limestone, drill for petroleum and natural gas, and cut sandstone.

Ohio's fertile farmland, mineral supplies, industries, and shipping ports provide many different kinds of work for Ohioans. The food and goods that these workers produce are used not only by other Ohioans but also by many people across the nation.

Protecting the Environment

The state's land has always provided food, shelter, and jobs for Ohioans. Rivers and streams water crops growing in the rich soil. Trees furnish wood for homes, furniture, and ships. The earth holds fuels such as coal and gas.

These natural resources have helped Ohio grow. Although the state is small, it has more industries than most other states its size. But the more Ohio's industries produce, the more they pollute the land. In fact, Ohio's industries have grown so much that they are poisoning the natural resources on which they depend.

Most industries produce waste materials that hold pollutants. Some of the waste is toxic, or poisonous. Over the years, Ohio's many industries have produced hundreds of millions of tons of **toxic waste**. In 1987 alone, industries in the state produced more than 666 million pounds (302 million kilograms) of toxic waste. Much of this waste goes into dumps or **landfills**, places where trash is buried.

Individuals have added to the problem, especially since the state's population has grown to more than 10 million residents. People create more toxic waste when they throw away toxic items such as paint, paint remover, and bug spray.

Landfills and dumps where toxic waste is found are called **hazardous waste sites.** Hazardous waste sites are dangerous because they produce toxic **leachate.** Leachate is rainwater that falls on toxic waste in landfills or dumps and absorbs the poisons that are in the waste.

If toxic leachate seeps into the ground, it can kill plants. It can also poison the **groundwater,** water beneath the ground that is tapped for drinking by almost half of all Ohioans. Some of the toxic leachate washes into rivers and streams, poisoning or killing fish and other wildlife. People who drink toxic water or eat poisoned fish can develop cancer or other illnesses.

There are more than 1,000 hazardous waste sites in Ohio. At least 400 of these sites are very likely to leak toxic waste or leachate.

At hazardous waste sites, barrels full of chemicals and other wastes can leak and pollute water and soil.

Collection programs, such as this one for paint, help keep hazardous waste out of landfills.

Ohioans are working to clean up these sites. Ohio is asking its citizens to reduce toxic waste by using fewer poisonous products. People can also help by bringing poisonous wastes to hazardous waste centers rather than throwing the materials into the trash.

The state government has set up strict laws for landfills. If industries put their toxic wastes into landfills, the landfills must be built specifically to hold toxic waste. All new landfills must have machines that collect and clean leachate. The landfills must also be lined with clay and plastic to keep leachate from seeping into the ground.

Not all Ohioans are happy about these laws, which make getting rid of toxic waste more difficult. The sealed landfills that meet the new regulations are more expensive to operate than the old landfills. When industries decide that Ohio's toxic-waste laws cost too much to follow, the industries sometimes move to states that have easier laws. Ohio then loses jobs and money.

Hazardous wastes such as nail polish, oven cleaner, and batteries are often dumped into landfills along with other garbage.

In some areas, pollution still flows into Ohio's water.

Ohioans must decide whether careless waste disposal is more harmful than unemployment. The Cuyahoga River is a reminder of how harmful toxic waste can be. The river was once so filled with oil and toxic wastes that it caught on fire. The fire forced industries and individuals to dispose of toxic wastes in safer ways. Since then, the Cuyahoga has gotten much cleaner, but wastes from factories and from hazardous waste sites still seep into the river. The Cuyahoga will not be completely healthy for many years.

The Cuyahoga River fire showed Ohioans that if industry and residents don't take care of toxic

60

Young Ohioans work to keep their environment healthy by checking for pollution in a stream.

waste, Ohio will become an unhealthy place to live and work. To prevent this from happening, many Ohioans are striving to make their state cleaner and safer for generations to come.

Ohio's Famous People

ACTORS & ENTERTAINERS

Clark Gable (1901–1960), born in Cadiz, Ohio, acted in more than 70 films, including *Mutiny on the Bounty* and *The Misfits*. Gable is probably best known for the role of Rhett Butler in *Gone with the Wind*.

▼ CLARK GABLE

▲ ARSENIO HALL

Arsenio Hall (born 1958) grew up in Cleveland. He hosted "The Arsenio Hall Show," a late-night talk show, and has co-starred in the movies *Coming to America* and *Harlem Nights*.

Annie Oakley (1860–1926) was an expert gunslinger who became famous for her performances with Buffalo Bill's Wild West show. Born in Darke County, Ohio, Oakley was so skilled with a gun that she could blast a cigarette out of a person's mouth without even scratching the person.

Steven Spielberg (born 1947) is a screenwriter, director, and producer from Cincinnati. His many successful movies include *E.T.: The Extra-Terrestrial*, *Raiders of the Lost Ark*, and *Schindler's List*.

▲ STEVEN SPIELBERG

ARTIST & MUSICIANS

TRACY ▶
CHAPMAN

Tracy Chapman (born 1964) is from Cleveland. She won three Grammy Awards for her first album, *Tracy Chapman*, which sold 10 million copies. She has performed in the Human Rights

62

Now! tour and in a march in honor of the Reverend Martin Luther King, Jr.

Maya Lin (born 1960) is a sculptor and an architect who designed the Vietnam Veterans' Memorial in Washington, D.C., and the Civil Rights Memorial in Montgomery, Alabama. Lin is a native of Athens, Ohio.

Joe Walsh (born 1947) grew up in Cleveland, where he began his music career with the James Gang. From 1976 to 1982, Walsh was a member of the Eagles. He performed on four of the group's albums, including *Hotel California* and *The Long Run*.

◀ MAYA LIN

JESSE OWENS ▶

▼ PETE ROSE

ATHLETES

Jesse Owens (1913–1980) moved to Cleveland at the age of seven. A star in track and field at Ohio State University, Owens won four gold medals at the 1936 Summer Olympic Games in Berlin, Germany. During his career, he broke seven world records.

Pete Rose (born 1941) played baseball for his hometown team, the Cincinnati Reds, and later became the team's manager. Rose is the all-time leading hitter in major-league baseball, with 4,256 hits. He was banned from baseball for gambling, or betting money, on the game.

Cy Young (1867–1955), of Gilmore, Ohio, was one of baseball's greatest pitchers. During his 21-year career in the major league he won a record 511 games. Young was elected to the Baseball Hall of Fame in 1937.

BUSINESS LEADERS

▼ RANSOM ELI OLDS

Harvey Firestone (1868–1938) started the Firestone Tire & Rubber Company in 1900. A native of Columbiana, Ohio, Firestone built his tire business in Akron. His company has grown to be one of the largest rubber tire producers in the world.

Ransom Eli Olds (1864–1950), of Geneva, Ohio, was an inventor and manufacturer of automobiles. He founded Olds Motor Works in 1899. The company built the first Oldsmobile two years later.

▲ HARVEY FIRESTONE

◀ **TECUMSEH**

DANIEL BEARD ▶

NATIVE AMERICAN LEADERS

Pontiac (1720–1769), an Ottawa Indian chief, united the Indian nations of the Great Lakes region to fight white settlers. In 1763 Pontiac and his warriors attacked British forts and settlements in what became known as Pontiac's War. He was born in northern Ohio.

Tecumseh (1768–1813) was a Shawnee chief from Old Piqua, Ohio, who worked to unite the Indians of the Ohio Valley. He encouraged tribespeople to fight to keep white settlers from taking the Indians' land. Tecumseh helped the British fight against American settlers in the War of 1812.

SOCIAL LEADERS

Daniel Beard (1850–1941), of Cincinnati, was a writer and outdoorsman. His boys' club, the Sons of Daniel Boone, merged with a group that came from Great Britain to become the Boy Scouts of America. He led the Boy Scouts for 31 years.

Branch Rickey (1881–1965) grew up near Toledo. Rickey was a baseball catcher, coach, manager, and executive. He signed on Jackie Robinson, the first African American to play baseball in the modern major leagues.

Gloria Steinem (born 1934) is a writer and an activist from Toledo. Since the 1960s, Steinem has worked for women's rights, civil rights, and global peace. She cofounded the magazines *New York* and *Ms.* and has written several books.

▼ GLORIA STEINEM

▲ BRANCH RICKEY

◀ PAUL DUNBAR

▲ TONI MORRISON

◀ JAMES THURBER

WRITERS

Paul Dunbar (1872–1906) was one of the first widely known black writers and one of the most popular American poets of his time. His books include *Lyrics of Lowly Life* and *The Sport of the Gods*. He was born in Dayton, Ohio.

Virginia Hamilton (born 1936) has written many award-winning books for young people, including *M. C. Higgins, the Great* and *Sweet Whispers, Brother Rush*. Hamilton's Ohio hometown, Yellow Springs, is a common setting for her stories, which are about the experiences of African-American children.

Toni Morrison (born 1931) from Lorain, Ohio, has written several books, including *Song of Solomon, Tar Baby, Beloved,* and *Jazz*. In 1993 Morrison became the first African American to win the Nobel Prize for literature.

James Thurber (1894–1961) gained fame writing humorous stories and drawing cartoons for the *New Yorker* magazine. Thurber's books include *The Thurber Carnival* and *The Wonderful O*. He was born in Columbus.

Facts-at-a-Glance

Nickname: Buckeye State
Song: "Beautiful Ohio"
Motto: With God, All Things Are Possible
Flower: scarlet carnation
Tree: buckeye
Bird: cardinal

Population: 10,847,115*
Rank in population, nationwide: 7th
Area: 44,828 sq mi (116,104 sq km)
Rank in area, nationwide: 34th
Date & ranking of statehood:
   March 1, 1803, the 17th state
Capital: Columbus
Major cities (and populations*):
   Columbus (632,910), Cleveland (505,616),
   Cincinnati (364,040), Toledo (332,943),
   Akron (223,019)
U.S. senators: 2
U.S. representatives: 19
Electoral votes: 21

Places to visit: Neil Armstrong Air & Space Museum in Wapakoneta, Pro Football Hall of Fame in Canton, Ohio Center of Science and Industry in Columbus, Aviation Trail in Dayton, Serpent Mound State Memorial in Adams County

Annual events: Buzzard Day in Hinckley (March), Festival of the Fish in Vermillion (June), Days of the Ships in Cleveland (June), Soap Box Derby in Akron (Aug.), Reynoldsburg Tomato Festival in Reynoldsburg (Sept.)

*1990 census

Average January temperature: 28° F (–2° C)	Average July temperature: 73° F (23° C)

Natural resources: fertile soil, coal, oil, natural gas, salt, clay, limestone, sandstone

Agricultural products: soybeans, corn, milk, beef cattle, hogs, poultry, tomatoes, apples, cucumbers, grapes

Manufactured goods: cars, aircraft parts, trucks, construction machinery, ovens, washing machines, chemicals, steel, rubber, clay, glass

ENDANGERED SPECIES

Mammals—Indiana bat, eastern wood rat, river otter, bobcat

Birds—dark-eyed junco, yellow-bellied sapsucker, sandhill crane, king rail, magnolia warbler

Fish—Ohio lamprey, cisco, longnose sucker, pirate perch, western banded killifish, shovelnose sturgeon

Plants—rock spikemoss, Appalachian quillwort, little gray polypody, threadlike naiad, reflexed bladder sedge, southern wood rush

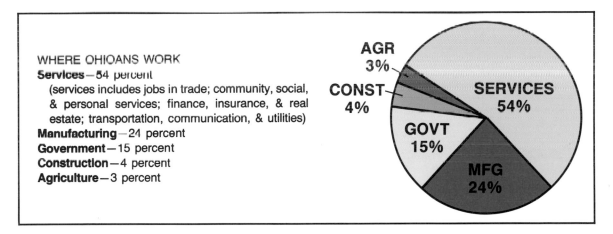

WHERE OHIOANS WORK

Services—54 percent
(services includes jobs in trade; community, social, & personal services; finance, insurance, & real estate; transportation, communication, & utilities)

Manufacturing—24 percent

Government—15 percent

Construction—4 percent

Agriculture—3 percent

AGR 3%
CONST 4%
SERVICES 54%
GOVT 15%
MFG 24%

PRONUNCIATION GUIDE

Akron (AK-ruhn)

Cincinnati (sihn-suh-NAT-ee)

Cuyahoga (ky-uh-HOH-guh)

Iroquois (IHR-uh-kwoy)

Marietta (mar-ee-EHT-uh)

Maumee (maw-MEE)

Muskingum (muh-SKIHNG-uhm)

Scioto (sy-OHT-uh)

Shawnee (shaw-NEE)

Tuscarawas (tuhs-kuh-RAW-uhs)

Wyandot (WY-uhn-daht)

colony A territory ruled by a country some distance away.

glacier A large body of ice and snow that moves slowly over land.

Great Lakes A chain of five lakes in Canada and the northern United States. They are Lakes Superior, Michigan, Huron, Erie, and Ontario.

groundwater Water that lies beneath the earth's surface. The water comes from rain and snow that seep through soil into the cracks and other openings in rocks. Groundwater supplies wells and springs.

hazardous waste site A collection point for used chemicals and other wastes that can harm living things or the environment. Hazardous wastes include materials that can poison, explode, burn flesh, start a fire, or carry disease.

landfill   A place specially prepared for burying waste.

leachate   Liquid that has seeped through waste or that forms when waste rots in a landfill. Leachate can contaminate water or soil.

plateau   A large, relatively flat area that stands above the surrounding land.

till   A mixture of clay, sand, and gravel dragged along by a glacier and left behind when the ice melts.

toxic waste   A poisonous material that contaminates the environment and that can cause death, disease, or other defects.

Underground Railroad   A system of escape routes that helped slaves get from the South to the North or Canada, where they would be free. Escaped slaves hid in homes and barns during the day and moved to the next safe place at night. The routes were not underground or part of a railroad, but railroad terms such as *station* and *conductor* were used as code words.

Index

Acknowledgments:

Maryland Cartographics, Inc., pp. 2, 10; Maslowski Photo, pp. 2–3, 17 (top); Lynn M. Stone, p. 6; Jack Lindstrom, p. 7; James Blank/Root Resources, pp. 8, 14, 42–43, 54; ODNR, pp. 11, 15, 16, 17 (bottom), 27 (bottom), 30, 41, 45, 48 (right), 52, 59, 61, 69; Kent & Donna Dannen, pp. 12, 19; Philip Wright/Visuals Unlimited, p. 13; The Cincinnati Historical Society, pp. 20, 29, 36; Michael J. Kabes, p. 21; Ohio Historical Society, pp. 22, 23, 25, 31, 37, 38, 65 (center left); Library of Congress, pp. 24, 28, 35; The St. Louis Mercantile Library, p. 26; Baus Collection, Roscoe Village Foundation, Inc., p. 27 (top); The Western Reserve Historical Society, Cleveland, Ohio, pp. 32–33, 33, 63 (bottom right), 65 (top left); Nesnadny & Schwartz, p. 44; David Liam Kyle/Cleveland Indians, p. 46; Cedar Point photo by Dan Feicht, p. 47; Monica V. Brown, Photographic Artist, p. 48 (left), 51, 71; GE Aircraft Engines, Cincinnati, Ohio, p. 49; Ohio Apple Marketing Program, p. 50; © 1992 Daniel E. Dempster, p. 53; Hans-Olaf Pfannkuch, p. 57 (left); Ohio Environmental Protection Agency, p. 57 (right); Information & Applied Communications, The Ohio State University, p. 58; S. Maslowski/Visuals Unlimited, p. 60; Hollywood Book and Poster, Inc., p. 62 (top right, top left, center, and bottom); Adam Stoltman, p. 63 (top right); Cincinnati Reds, p. 63 (bottom left); *Dictionary of American Portraits*, p. 64 (top right and left, bottom left); The Ohioana Library, p. 64 (bottom right); Joseph Marzullo, Retna Ltd., p. 65 (top right); © Maria Mulas, p. 65 (center right); Douglas Glass, p. 65 (bottom); Jean Matheny, p. 66.